CELEBRATING THE CITY OF RIYADH

Celebrating the City of Riyadh

Walter the Educator

Silent King Books

SILENT KING BOOKS

SKB

RIYADH

In the heart of the desert, where the sands shift and gleam,

Celebrating the City of
Riyadh

Celebrating the City of Riyadh is a little collectible souvenir book that belongs to the Celebrating Cities Book Series by Walter the Educator. Collect them all and more books at WaltertheEducator.com

USE THE EXTRA SPACE TO TAKE NOTES AND DOCUMENT YOUR MEMORIES

Lies Riyadh, a city born from an ancient dream.

A realm of modern marvels where tradition holds sway,

A tapestry of history woven with the threads of to-day.

From the whispers of the past in Diriyah's old stone,

To the gleaming skyscrapers that Riyadh calls its own,

A metropolis of contrasts, where the old meets the new,

To the gleaming skyscrapers that Riyadh calls its own,

A metropolis of contrasts, where the old meets the new,

In the heart of Arabia, a city that grew.

Celebrating the City of
Riyadh

The morning sun rises, casting golden light,

On bustling markets that awaken with the night.

Al-Zal Market hums with merchants' vibrant cries,

Where spices and perfumes dance under open skies.

Palms sway gently, a respite from the heat,

Their shadows a sanctuary for weary feet.

In King Abdullah Park, laughter fills the air,

Families gather, moments of joy to share.

Riyadh's pulse quickens as the city awakes,

Celebrating the City of

Riyadh

The rhythm of life in every step it takes.

From Olaya's thoroughfares, alive and astir,

To the quieter corners where memories blur.

In the shadow of Al Faisaliyah, a spire of grace,

Reflecting the aspirations of a nation's embrace,

A symbol of progress piercing the sky,

Guiding the future with a watchful eye.

Kingdom Centre's pinnacle touches the stars,

A testament to ambition that knows no bars.

Celebrating the City of
Riyadh

Its archway a gateway to dreams unfurled,

A beacon of hope to the whole wide world.

In the halls of Masmak Fort, history stands still,

Echoes of warriors, a testament to will.

The cradle of a kingdom, where unity was sown,

In every brick and stone, a story well-known.

Riyadh's heartbeat resonates in each souq and mall,

Where cultures converge in a vibrant thrall.

A melting pot of languages, flavors, and art,

Where East meets West in a global heart.

Beneath the city's streets, a network unseen,

The Riyadh Metro, sleek and clean.

A promise of connectivity, a bridge to the new,

Streamlining the pathways for dreams to pursue.

Celebrating the City of

Riyadh

ABOUT THE CREATOR

Walter the Educator is one of the pseudo-nyms for Walter Anderson. Formally educated in Chemistry, Business, and Education, he is an educator, an author, a diverse entrepreneur, and he is the son of a disabled war veteran. "Walter the Educator" shares his time between educating and creating. He holds interests and owns several creative projects that entertain, enlighten, enhance, and educate, hoping to inspire and motivate you. Follow, find new works, and stay up to date with Walter the Educator™ at WaltertheEducator.com.

Printed in Great Britain
by Amazon